Independent Schools
Examinations Board

English Practice Exercises 13+
Answer Book

Amanda Alexander
and
Rachel Gee

Independent Schools
Examinations Board

www.galorepark.co.uk

GALORE PARK

Published by ISEB Publications, an imprint of Galore Park Publishing Ltd
19/21 Sayers Lane, Tenterden, Kent TN30 6BW
www.galorepark.co.uk

Layout by Typetechnique

Printed by Replika Press, India

ISBN: 978 1 907047 169

First published 2009, printed edition 2010, 2011, 2012

Details of other ISEB Revision Guides for Common Entrance, examination
papers and Galore Park publications are available at www.galorepark.co.uk

Contents

Introduction

We hope that this answer book will be a useful tool for teachers and parents using and marking English Practice Exercises 13+.

The grid format of the answers to the Reading Paper texts is modelled on the ISEB mark schemes as is the allocation of marks. We hope that you find this detailed analysis a time-saver: the main quotes, key features and writing techniques have all been carefully identified. This is a starting point for marking, suggested rather than prescriptive, as it is not possible to write a hard and fast mark scheme for English, unlike other subjects. We acknowledge that children often discover the unusual and that teachers prefer the autonomy to mark in their own way.

The grids for marking the Writing Paper contain the descriptors provided by the ISEB. The marking of children's writing is even more subjective but these provide a guide on the allocation of marks.

Teachers may wish to use this set of answers themselves. Alternatively, it may be preferable for children to have their own copy, at the marking stage, to have a better understanding of what is required and so improve their marks; it will also give parents the same assistance.

These answers have been trialled with our Year 8 pupils.

We extend our thanks to them and to our Editor Andrew Hammond, and Nicholas Oulton at Galore Park.

Amanda Alexander and Rachel Gee
November 2008

Resources

For further guidance on how to structure an answer for the 13+ English examination pupils and parents will find the following helpful, available from Galore Park www.galorepark.co.uk:

English ISEB Revision Guide by Susan Elkin   ISBN 978 0 903627 57 3

Paper 1: Reading
Section A: Non-fiction

The following pages provide guidance on marking Exercises 1A.1 to 1A.10

Exercise 1A.1

Thura's Diary: My Life in Wartime Iraq by Thura al-Windari

Q	Answer	Mark	Additional Guidance
1.	*Answers could refer to:* • simile: 'it feels … burning building' – feeling of choking in enclosed space • personification: 'hurt the soil' – power of rain to cause injury • personification: 'Mother Nature is depressed and in pain.' – all natural things affected by smoke and rain	4	Best candidates will identify, recognise and explain two examples of imagery.
2.	*Look for references to:* • personal pronouns / direct appeal: 'I leave my story in your safekeeping' – dedicated to reader • repetition: 'a girl' begins many phrases – keeps focus on her experiences • third person: 'a girl' – she is one of many, big picture to personal impact • emotive language: 'exploding', 'cruel sanctions', 'terrified', 'scared' – conveys fear • 'but a girl … hope' – contrast with fear	4	*Marker's discretion* Fewer points should be dealt with in detail. More points could be covered in less detail.
3.	*Answers should refer to:* • first entry mood: hopeless • 'we are drowning in this polluted … world' – unable to see any way out • second entry mood: hopeful • 'the future is shining … like a bright light' – not giving up	6	*Marker's discretion* Award marks for insight and explanation of moods, and relevance of supporting quotes.

Q		Answer	Mark	Additional Guidance
4.		*Answers could include:* • observant: 'the sky turns … fire-engine red' • sympathetic/caring: 'Poor Aula and Mum … to the dust' • resigned: 'We are drowning … dusty world' • ambitious: 'get myself to America …' • forgiving: 'not to take revenge' • hopeful: 'The future … bright light' • philosophical: 'all live together … us' • idealistic: 'while there's still life … completely' • brave: refer to whole text	6	Candidates should refer to two or three impressions. The best candidates will display ability to quote with relevance, and explain clearly in their own words.
5.	(a) (b)	• this is a hopeful message for the world *Look for references to:* • goes beyond personal recount • sums up experiences/not daily • readership widened • message to the world • future tense: future hope • change of font/writing style	1 4	Award 1 mark. *Marker's discretion* Award up to 4 marks for answers which prove an understanding of typical/non-typical features of diary writing.
TOTAL			25	

Exercise 1A.2

'The Love of a Dog' by George Graham Vest from *Speeches that Changed the World*

Q	Answer	Mark	Additional Guidance
1.	Section 1: • people/family may be unreliable/turn away • money may be lost • reputation may be lost • people might be fickle/disloyal Section 2: • dog stays with you in sickness and health • good times and bad • loyalty and protection of dog • whatever circumstances • even until death	6	Award up to 3 marks for the summary of each section. Award 1 mark for each point, which displays overall understanding of both sections.
2.	• man's inadequacies makes a dog's attributes more appealing • strong ending	2	Candidates should refer to one in detail or both in less detail, or any other appropriate idea.
3.	• metaphor: 'when riches take wings' – take off financially • metaphor: 'reputation falls to pieces' – reputation is lost • simile: 'as constant in his love as the sun in its journey' – night and day without fail • personification: 'sun in its journey' – time passing	6	Look for three examples plus explanation/comment. Good candidates will identify and recognise examples of imagery.

Q	Answer	Mark	Additional Guidance
4.	*Answers could identify:* • emotive vocabulary: 'faithful and true even in death' – shock value • playing on guilt: 'The one absolutely unselfish friend ... selfish world' • appealing to the reader: 'those whom we trust' – draws the listener in • alliteration: 'wintry winds' – for emphasis • repetition: of 'The one ...' – impact • cluster/rule of three: 'an outcast ... homeless' – impact	6	Three examples plus explanations are needed. Good candidates will identify, recognise and explain persuasive techniques.
5.	*Answers may make reference to:* • own experience/knowledge • information, or lack of, in the speech • structure • language	5	*Marker's discretion* Highest marks will go to candidates who cover a range of points and support their opinion clearly with some reference to the text.
TOTAL		25	

Exercise 1A.3

Born Survivor by Bear Grylls

Q	Answer	Mark	Additional Guidance
1.	*Answers should refer to:* • personification: 'faces' – different types of sea • personification: 'strip ... hope' – feeling demoralised/exposed	4	Award up to 2 marks for each. Identification, recognition and explanation necessary.
2.	*Answers could refer to:* • water all around but unobtainable • food near but unable to bring aboard • ships that pass but could not be heard • redemption	5	Good candidates will find and summarise four points. Best candidates will express ideas clearly.
3.	*Answers should include:* • metaphor: 'stripping away ... blanket' – comfort and safety have been removed • irrelevance of status – explain in own words • personification: 'sea ... reduce you' – power of the sea to demoralise	6	Award up to 2 marks for each of three points. Best candidates will demonstrate ability to quote and explain in their own words.
4.	*Answers could make reference to:* food: • rope used as fishing line • torch spring used to make nails and hooks • knife made from a biscuit tin, which he used to gut fish • ate seagulls • caught a shark drink: • rain water collected from tarpaulin/life jacket, sucked seagull's blood and bones	6	Award 4 marks for four well-explained references to food. Award 2 marks for two well-explained references to drink.

Q	Answer	Mark	Additional Guidance
5.	*Answers could include:* different: • Bear Grylls chose to be an explorer • Poon Lim was a Chinese sailor serving on a British cargo ship and this was his job similar: • the sea is still as dangerous • the same challenges are faced	4	Award up to 2 marks for clear expression of differences. Award up to 2 marks for clear expression of similarities.
TOTAL		**25**	

Exercise 1A.4

'The Need for Adventure' adapted from the Patrick Hardy Lecture given by Anthony Horowitz, November 2005

Q	Answer	Mark	Additional Guidance
1.	*Answers could refer to:* • controversial topic: 'hot topic' – of interest to all • rhetorical questions: 'Do boys read?' – draws reader in • short sentences: 'I feel strongly about that.' – impact • shock: 'violence in children's books … isn't enough of it' – not expected	4	Award marks for identification and explanation of two ways in which attention is gained.
2.	*Answers should refer to:* • simile: 'books … like doors', 'open like doors' – allows you to enter in • extended imagery: 'go through a door' • extended metaphor: 'whole world on the other side' – books transport you	4	Best candidates will recognise that door/book imagery builds/extends. Award up to 4 marks for identification, recognition and full understanding of at least two images.
3.	Answers may refer to: language: • impact: repetition of 'scared' • includes the reader: repetition of 'we' • use of words 'for'/'of' – to change meaning of 'scared' sentence structure: • thinking aloud – 'No. It's worse that that.' • short, sharp, shock effect – 'Our children inspire fear.'	4	Award up to 2 marks for language and 2 for sentence structures. Reward answers which identify, recognise and understand the author's craft.
4.	*Answers may refer to:* • thinks children need/want to read about violence • fearful society/not as much freedom • adventure always crucial for him • always told stories • discovered reading enjoyment • influence of James Bond	6	*Marker's discretion* Fewer reasons should be dealt with in detail. More reasons could be covered in less detail.

Q	Answer	Mark	Additional Guidance
5.	*Answers may refer to:* • at first concerned that she saw his books as vehicle to better authors • then accepts and is pleased that his books encourage and extend children's reading	4	Best candidates will understand and explain his changed reaction.
6.	*Answers should include:* • reading is the greatest adventure, allowing the reader to experience new worlds and challenges	3	Reward candidates who interpret statement fully.
TOTAL		**25**	

Exercise 1A.5

'Morocco' by Andrew Gilchrist from *The Guardian*, 10th November 2001

Q	Answer	Mark	Additional Guidance
1.	*Answers could include:* • alliteration/assonance: 'back of a battered …' – ugly sounds drawn together • metaphor: 'bouncy castle on wheels' – travelling along and being thrown up and down • metaphor: 'limb-dislocating' – emphasizes roughness • alliteration: 'golden sand glimmering' – repeated 'g' sound emphasises both words	4	Best candidates will refer to one use of imagery and one sound device. Identification, recognition and explanation is necessary for both.
2.	*Answers may include:* • sights: 'pale western sun worshippers', 'brightly-painted old quarters' • sounds: 'haggling in the bazaars', 'jostling, deafening flow' • tastes: 'delicious … spiced up' • feelings/touch: 'bouncy castle on wheels', 'limb dislocating', 'jostling'	6	Candidates should identify the use of up to three senses. Reward candidates who select fresh quotes that support opening statement.
3.	*Look for references to:* • use of lists – overwhelming information: 'hassle … haggling', 'hustlers, and conmen' • activities and people not familiar to us: 'hassle … haggling', 'maelstrom … medinas' • alliteration/impact of strong vocabulary: 'desperate and dying'	4	Candidates should comment on two devices and explain their impact.
4.	*Answers could refer to:* • anxious: 'limb dislocating' • overwhelmed: 'big-time culture shock' • impressed: 'kaleidoscopic maze … mosques' • excited: 'It's no great worry … half the fun'	6	*Marker's discretion* Award marks for insight/ explanation and supporting quotes of at least two feelings.

Q	Answer	Mark	Additional Guidance
5.	• travel/persuasion/journalistic/informative *Answers may refer to:* • paints pictures: 'little boats nodding inshore', 'ramparts straddling the rocks' • uses the senses: 'lapped by big noisy waves', 'caught up … flow' • lists: information given quickly • strong verbs: 'lapped', 'straddling', 'swaying', 'swaddled' • addresses the reader/direct appeal: 'wander in and just get caught up' • pronouns: 'little French you can … school' • a land of contrasts: beach/city, old/new, peaceful/noisy, familiar/unfamiliar	5	Award 1 mark. Award up to 4 marks to candidates who support their opinions with at least two reasons and explanations based on evidence from this text.
TOTAL		**25**	

Exercise 1A.6

'Queuing' by Christopher Middleton from *The Daily Telegraph*, 26th September 2005

Q		Answer	Mark	Additional Guidance
1.	(a)	*Answers could include:* • content: manners/old versus young generation • techniques: alliteration, assonance, pun	2	Up to 2 marks for impact of headline.
	(b)	• explanation of choice	2	Up to 2 marks for justification of choice.
2.		• wildebeests represent OAPs • river crocodiles represent children *Look for references to:* • image created – vulnerable OAPs over-run by the fit and strong predators, snapping at their heels in order to get to their food	3	*Marker's discretion* Highest marks will go to candidates who understand and explain the comparison in detail.
3.	(a)	• bank window and train ticket office	2	Award 2 marks.
	(b)	• blood-pressure-raising: answer reflects understanding of situation e.g. as always seem to be behind the slowest person/ wish another queue	2	Award 2 marks for two episodes well-explained.
4.		Answers could include: • he thinks they are rude • pushing in with no consideration for others • Class 6B on way home for tea on No. 97 bus pushing others out of the way • they are independent/they don't follow the crowd/not bound by tradition/get what they want quickly • going to automatic cash machine with no queue rather than joining longer queue	4	Award up to 2 marks for view and explanation with example. Award up to 2 marks for contrasting view and explanation with example.

Q	Answer	Mark	Additional Guidance
5.	*Answers could refer to:* • humour: tells cash dispenser story against himself • imagery: 'wildebeest', 'river crocodiles', 'scurried rat-like' • familiar to all: bus queue, David Attenborough, 'proceed to counter No. 4' • anecdotes: train tickets, bank queue	6	*Marker's discretion* Fewer points should be dealt with in detail. More points could be covered in less detail.
6.	*Answers could include:* • proud to be British/enjoys tradition • watches TV/likes wildlife • frustrated at breakdown of order • can laugh at himself • maintain standards at whatever cost	4	There should be at least two well-explained comments with supporting evidence.
TOTAL		**25**	

Exercise 1A.7

**The first review of *Harry Potter and the Order of the Phoenix*
by Leo Lewis from *Timesonline*, 28th June 2007**

Q		Answer	Mark	Additional Guidance
1.		*Answers may refer to:* Tokyo • colour: bright lights/flashing cameras • time: modern/city setting Hogwarts • colour: grey/drab • time: old/castle setting	4	Candidates should find two contrasting points.
2.	(a)	*Look for references to:* • British talent/British author/Hollywood provided magic	3	Candidates should refer to all three points.
	(b)	• money-making/to boost viewing/ publicity and profits	1	Candidates should recognise financial gain.
3.		*Answers should refer to:* • children are weak/lack depth and subtlety • adults are strong/believable • inexperience may account for difference	3	Award up to 2 marks for summary, which proves understanding. Award 1 mark.
4.		*Answers should include:* • personification: 'joyful little glimpses' – causes great happiness • alliteration: 'wizarding world' – draws the words together for impact • alliteration: 'punctuated and perked' – draws the words together for impact • metaphor: 'punctuated and perked' brings life to image • metaphor: 'furniture ... punctuated' – necessary items to fill spaces	6	Candidates should identify, recognise and explain two writing techniques.

Q		Answer	Mark	Additional Guidance
5.	(a)	*Answers may refer to:* liked: • adult actors • movement between school and modern retail setting • necessary milestone in saga disliked: • child actors • shortage of glimpses of school life • turgid/lacked pace • still a long way to go until end of saga	6	Candidates must refer to likes and dislikes. Award up to 3 marks for each summary, which proves understanding.
	(b)	• overall a good film but disappointing in parts	2	Award 2 marks for a well-expressed answer.
TOTAL			**25**	

Exercise 1A.8

Long Walk to Freedom: The Autobiography of Nelson Mandela by Nelson Mandela

Q		Answer	Mark	Additional Guidance
1.	(a) (b) (c)	*Look for references to:* • carefree, taken for granted • wanted freedom to do what he wanted, boyhood freedom not the reality • to lead lawful and fulfilled life	6	Award up to 2 marks for each summary.
2.	(a) (b)	*Answers should refer to:* • wanted freedom for all • oppressed to be liberated • oppressor to be liberated	1 3	Award 1 mark. Award up to 3 marks for clear explanation of both points.
3.	(a) (b)	*Answers should refer to:* • to extend the metaphor from earlier in the sentence • 'first step' – just the beginning • 'longer … difficult road' – difficult task/ journey to be free/understand/improve freedom of others	1 3	Best candidates will recognise extended metaphor. Award up to 3 marks for metaphorical understanding of 'step' and 'road' and explanation of journey.
4.		*Answers could include:* • use of first person/personal pronoun: 'I was not born … free' • whole life experiences described: 'for my long walk is not yet ended' • detail/anecdote: 'free to roast mealies … slow-moving bulls' • views/opinions: 'to liberate the oppressed and the oppressor both'	6	Award up to 6 marks for identification and explanation of three features of writing.

Q	Answer	Mark	Additional Guidance
5.	*Answers could refer to:* • metaphor: 'I have walked ... freedom' – long journey/dedicated his life to the pursuit of freedom for all • metaphor: 'I have tried not to falter' – tried not to make mistakes along the way/determined • metaphor: 'climbing a great hill' – personal achievement/steadfast • metaphor: 'many more hills to climb' – wants to achieve more, won't give up • metaphor: 'steal a view of the glorious vista' – looking back over life's achievements, reflective • metaphor: 'dare not linger' – no time to rest, perseverance	5	Best candidates will identify and explain at least two contrasting examples of imagery and will show an understanding of Nelson Mandela's qualities.
TOTAL		25	

Exercise 1A.9

'A Giant Problem' by Martin Hickman from *The Independent*, 27th February 2006

Q	Answer	Mark	Additional Guidance
1.	*Answers could include:* • strong/emotive vocabulary: 'hulking grey box' • cluster of three/rhetorical questions: 'what do you do … widescreen betters?' • contrast of old and new: 'hulking grey box', 'sleek exciting new Apple' • pronouns: 'What do you do with your old telly … ?'	6	*Marker's discretion* Two points should be dealt with in detail. More points could be covered in less detail.
2.	*Answers could refer to:* • 'dump these once treasured items': makes you think about what you throw away and why – irresponsible • monosyllabic words: 'in the bin, the tip': – quickly discarded – as if you don't care • emotive language: 'poison the ground' – guilt • impact: 'lost to future generations' – guilt • refer to contrast: 'jettison items once so coveted' – awareness	4	Best candidates will find two different feelings supported with quotes.
3. (a)	*Answers should include:* • use of statistics/image of jumbo jets to persuade • all could be recycled so should not fill sites	2	Candidates should refer to both points.
(b)	• the Government slow response unlike other EU countries	1	Award 1 mark.

Q	Answer	Mark	Additional Guidance
4.	*Answers should refer to:* • Government to introduce new European rules as many other EU countries • neighbourhood collection sites like bottle banks and municipal dumps • consumers return goods to retailer to play a part in collection and recycling • consumer be more responsible in buying new and repairing	6	Highest marks will go to candidates who refer to Government, retailer and consumer. Candidates should base their ideas on the text and express themselves clearly.
5.	*Answers could touch on reasons such as:* • throw away society • goods are cheap so throw away rather than repair • fashion – want latest model • Government not proactive enough	6	Award up to 6 marks for three well-reasoned points.
TOTAL		**25**	

Exercise 1A.10

From *As I Walked Out One Midsummer Morning* by Laurie Lee

Q	Answer	Mark	Additional Guidance
1.	*Answers could include:* • nervous: 'I felt tense and shaky.' • isolated: 'nakedly apart' • surprised: 'neither arrested ... shut up.' • elated: 'it seemed too easy' • growing confidence: 'gradually acquiring the truths of the trade' • excitement: 'it became a greedy pleasure'	4	Award 4 marks to candidates who provide two moods with these or other supporting quotes and explanations.
2.	*Look for references to:* sights: • simile: 'like a gun' – needs protection • metaphor: 'stood nakedly apart' – feeling exposed • cluster of three: 'my back to the wall ... violin under my chin.' – setting information imparted quickly • contrast: 'part of the hurrying crowds ... apart' crowd/alone sounds: • onomatopoeia: 'trains rattling' – sound effects of train	6	Three points should be made to include sights and sounds and explanations.
3. (a) (b)	*Summaries should refer to:* • using the hat and choice of tune *Answers could include:* • playing slow melodies/as well as you can/ appealing tunes/measured enthusiasm	2 3	References to both are necessary. Award 3 points for using own words or using quotes.

Q	Answer	Mark	Additional Guidance
4.	*Look for references to:* • 'greedy pleasure' – enjoys playing like a hungry man eating (metaphor) • 'sawing away' – in abandoned enthusiasm (metaphor) • 'moony melody' – soft 'm' (alliteration) • 'a kind of obsession' – can't stop playing (powerful vocabulary) • 'gold dust fever' – comparison with gold diggers (metaphor) • 'tips of my fingers burned' – emphasising frantic playing (metaphor)	4	Best candidates will quote, recognise and fully explain two points.
5.	*Answers could include:* • resourceful: 'went out … try my luck' • determined: 'I must face it now' • courageous: started playing although 'tense and shaky' • observant: 'acquiring the truths … trade' • honest: 'too easy, like a confidence trick' • musical: ability to play a range of tunes	6	Candidates should refer to three impressions including explanation using quotes and own words.
TOTAL		25	

21

Paper 1: Reading
Section B: Poetry

The following pages provide guidance on marking Exercises 1B.1 to 1B.10

Exercise 1B.1

'Space Shot' by Gareth Owen

Q		Answer	Mark	Additional Guidance
1.	(a) (b)	• rocket/spacecraft *References should be made to:* • awe/amazement • size/ability to fly	1 2	Award 1 mark. Award 2 marks.
2.		*Answers could include:* sights: • metaphor: 'out of the furnace' – as if rising out of flames • metaphor: 'great fish' – shape and colour • metaphor extended: 'silver tail on fire' – colour and flames • simile: 'but with a slowness like something sorry to be rid of earth' – reluctance to leave earth's safety • metaphor: 'boiling mountains' – emphasises enormity of vapour • personification: 'search for a space' – small compared to sky sounds: • metaphor/onomatopoeia: 'ground thundered/With a roar' – sound effects • onomatopoeia: 'teacups/Rattling' – reproduces sound of vibrations	8	Four examples in total to include at least one sight and one sound, with explanation. Best candidates will identify, recognise and explain choices.
3.		*Answers could refer to:* • sense of awe • enormity of event • fear/excitement at noise/trembling ground • bright/vivid colours – tinted glasses needed • interest in space exploration/scientific phenomenon	4	Award full marks to candidates who explain two points with clarity, and show a clear personal response.

Q	Answer	Mark	Additional Guidance
4.	*Look for references to:* • 'unknown universe' – mystery of space • 'waited', 'waiting' – exploration hasn't happened yet – will it ever happen in the future? • 'always been good at' – never been challenged as wonder of space too great for man to explore	4	*Marker's discretion* Best answers will display full understanding, insight and clarity.
5.	*Answers could include:* • attempt – having a shot • snapshot/video shot – a moment in time • space shot – spacecraft pierces the sky • space shot – space will be shot/broken by the spacecraft • gunshot – like a bullet firing from a gun	6	Highest marks will go to candidates who can explain two interpretations in detail.
TOTAL		25	

Exercise 1B.2

'Blessing' by Imtiaz Dharker

Q	Answer	Mark	Additional Guidance
1.	*Answers could include:* • alliteration: 'small splash' – draws words together for emphasis • onomatopoeia: 'echo' – sound effect • metaphor: 'kindly god' – significance • vocabulary: 'tin mug' – simplistic and childlike	6	Three examples needed to include identification, recognition and explanation. Good candidates will recognise and explain the emphasis.
2.	• 'The skin cracks like a pod.' – simile – emphasises dryness • 'the liquid sun' – metaphor – pulls water and sun together • 'highlights polished to perfection' – metaphor/alliteration – effect of sun • 'the blessing sings' – personification – power of water emphasised	4	Identify techniques used and explain effect of two of them.
3.	• irregular *Answers should refer to:* • pod/god – draws those six lines together/ rounds off • ground/found/around – emphasises steady flow of water	5	Award 1 mark. Award 2 marks. Award 2 marks.
4. (a) (b)	• first two lines: short sentences to show the topic/factual statement • remainder: long descriptive sentences and use of enjambment/caesura *Answers could include* • short sentences: create shock • short sentences: state facts • longer sentences: suggest flow of water • longer sentences: describe activity and events	3 3	Award 2 marks to candidates who refer to sentence structures. Full marks gained if candidates name poetic techniques. *Marker's discretion* Marks can be given according to understanding of the structure.

Q	Answer	Mark	Additional Guidance
5.	*Answers should refer to:* • the gift of water is a blessing: a free gift • irony: the burst pipe is not a blessing long-term – too much water at once/ uses up supplies	4	Full marks for candidates who refer to both points and explain them in their own words in a clear and detailed way.
TOTAL		25	

Exercise 1B.3

'To Sleep' by William Wordsworth

Q		Answer	Mark	Additional Guidance
1.	(a)	*Answer should refer to:* • his attempt to get off to sleep	1	Award 1 mark.
	(b)	sight: • 'a flock of sheep' • 'the fall of rivers' • 'winds and seas' • 'smooth fields' • 'pure sky' sound: • 'rain and bees murmuring'	2	One sight and one sound to be recognised.
2.	(a)	*Answers should make reference to:* octet: • how he has tried to sleep • still sleepless • hears the dawn chorus	3	Three short summaries necessary for 3 marks.
	(b)	sestet: • similar pattern of poor sleep in previous nights • appeals to 'sleep' • importance of sleep and why	3	Three short summaries necessary for 3 marks.
3.		*Answers should include:* rhythm: • pentameter – usual sonnet form • moves it on/comforting/predictable • wishes his sleep could have this steady rhythm • some use of enjambment for flow rhyme: • abba x 2 in octet • cdcdcd in sestet – denounces change between sestet and octet • rhyme moves reader on to ends of lines	6	Rhythm: three well-explained points are necessary. Best candidates will recognise pentameter. Rhyme: three well-explained points are necessary.

Q		Answer	Mark	Additional Guidance
4.	(a)	*Look for references to:* • is the break between night and day • allows thought and health	2	2 marks for reference to both points.
	(b)	• use of imperative to appeal: 'come blessed barrier' • metaphor: 'blessed barrier' – emphasises welcome necessity of sleep to break night and day • personification: 'Dear mother' – power of sleep to renew as if reborn • personification: 'joyous health' – celebration of well being	4	Good candidates will identify, recognise and explain two poetic techniques/writing features.
5.		*Answers could include:* exclamation marks: • 'Come blessed barrier … health!', 'And could not win thee, sleep!' – shows frustration and urgency question marks: • 'Without thee … wealth?' – impact on reader/poet's further frustration and questioning colons and semi colons: • emphasise broken stream of consciousness	4	Award 4 marks to candidates who show detailed understanding of two different examples of punctuation.
TOTAL			25	

Exercise 1B.4

'Clown' by Phoebe Hesketh

Q	Answer	Mark	Additional Guidance
1.	*References should be made to:* • how: make up – 'whitened face/and red nose' • why: to protect self – 'Hidden away from himself'	3	Award 1 mark for 'how' and 2 marks for 'why'.
2.	jackets have literal meaning: • wearing inside out • torn and patched troubles are metaphorical: • turning our troubles 'inside out' – covering them up • 'wearing our rents and patches' – temporarily taking his audience's troubles	6	Award 2 marks for literal understanding. Award up to 4 marks for metaphorical understanding. Good candidates will recognise and explain use of imagery.
3.	*Answers should identify:* • cheers up his audience 'cheer and heal', 'make us laugh' • makes his audience feel superior 'he made us feel tall', 'we knew we could cope'	6	Award up to 3 marks for each. Candidates should refer to two ways and explain them in their own words and with close reference to the text.
4.	*Answers could include:* • metaphor: 'tightrope he walked' – narrow existence • personification: 'when the laughter died' – needs the prop of being laughed at • metaphor: 'nowhere to hide in the empty night' – no escape from his thoughts • metaphor: 'catch fall' – save him from loneliness/protect him	6	Three examples to include identification, recognition and explanation. *Marker's discretion* Award marks according to detail, clarity and insight of answer.

Q	Answer	Mark	Additional Guidance
5.	*Answers could make reference to:* • theme/subject change: the real man • emphasis on clown's life	4	Candidates should recognise and explain the theme/subject change. Candidates should also recognise that the new stanza emphasises this.
TOTAL		**25**	

Exercise 1B.5

'Hawk Roosting' by Ted Hughes

Q	Answer	Mark	Additional Guidance
1.	*Answers should identify:* • the convenience: 'air's buoyancy and the sun's ray', 'earth's face upward'	4	For full marks candidates should refer to two advantages with supporting quote and explanation, or write in their own words.
2.	*Answers should make reference to:* • Creation – the god/maker who made him • Creation – the whole world at his disposal • use of capital – reference to God's Creation	5	Award 2 marks for each of the two points made with explanation. Award 1 mark for understanding the use of the capital letter.
3.	• allotment – hawk's choice who dies – his power • allotment – the place of death – the setting	4	For full marks candidates should understand and explain both meanings of the word.
4.	*Answers could include:* • strong statements: 'Nothing has changed since I began' – all powerful • use of personal pronouns: 'I kill where I please' – emphasises hawk's belief in himself • personification: 'earth's face … inspection' – reduces importance of the earth to human status, hawk's power greater • metaphor: 'hold Creation', 'revolve' – hawk's ability and power emphasised • emotive vocabulary: 'tearing off heads' – shock of cruelty of hawk	8	Four examples to include identification, recognition and explanation. Many possible quotes: good candidates will select best examples.

Q	Answer	Mark	Additional Guidance
5.	Look for references to: • hawk • power • creation • destruction • arrogance • overview	4	Award up to 2 marks for a title that proves good understanding. Award up to 2 marks for clear and supported explanation of ideas.
TOTAL		**25**	

Exercise 1B.6

'Toad' by Norman MacCaig

Q	Answer	Mark	Additional Guidance
1. (a)	*Answers should refer to:* • simile • colour and leathery texture • shape: malleable and old-fashioned clip purse • containing a jewel	3	1 mark for recognition of simile. Award up to 2 marks for two points to explain comparison.
(b)	• not to be so inanimate/like a 'thing'	1	Award 1 mark.
2.	*Answers could include:* • 'clamber' – meaning and sound • 'right…foot' – steady slow rhythm • simile: 'like a Japanese wrestler' – hunched wide stance	6	Best candidates should quote and explain all three points in detail.
3.	*Reference could be made to:* • use of purse – metaphor • hand meant for the purse • hand moulds to the shape of a purse – the toad	3	*Marker's discretion* Fewer points should be dealt with in detail. More points could be covered in less detail.
4.	*Answers could make reference to:* • beautiful for the poet despite ugliness • 'A jewel in your head?' – rhetorical question • 'you've put one in mine' – answer to question • 'tiny radiance in dark place' – contrast of radiance with dark	4	Best candidates will understand the overall meaning: the beauty of toad.

Q		Answer	Mark	Additional Guidance
5.	(a)	*Look for references to:* structure: • stanzas 1/3/5 contain thoughts • stanzas 2/4 contain events number of lines per stanza: • 1/3/5 are three lines • 2/4 are two lines with exception of 'every star' – emphasis	4	Award up to 4 marks for detailed understanding of content and stanza line lengths.
	(b)	*References should be made to:* punctuation: • use of questions – involves reader • use of capitals/enjambment/caesura – broken rhythm mirrors awkward movement of toad	4	Award highest marks to candidates who recognise and explain rhetorical question and enjambment/ caesura.
TOTAL			**25**	

Exercise 1B.7

'An Old Woman' by R S Thomas

Q	Answer	Mark	Additional Guidance
1.	*References could include:* • measure of routine: daily pattern of drawing water – 'pails of water, … pump' • liquid measure: making tea – 'drops of milkless tea …' • measure of time passing relentlessly: 'Yet neither tea …', 'in the grate' • measure of inevitable physical ageing: 'ice that forms … veins', 'knots the blood', 'clouds the clear, blue eye'	6	Best candidates will interpret and explain use of 'measure' in at least two ways with supporting quotes. Reward understanding.
2.	*Answers could include:* • metaphor: 'crop of faces' – children's faces like growing flowers • extended metaphor: 'blooming' – suggests healthiness, growing number of faces • alliteration: 'curious children cluster' – interesting words pulled together for emphasis • assonance: 'cluster in the dusk' – repetition of soft 'u'	6	Candidates should identify, recognise and explain two or three examples depending on detail.
3.	*Answers may refer to:* • routine life: 'her days are measured out' • near to death: 'her days are measured' • ageing physically: 'knots the blood', 'Vision being weak … age.' • frail/small: 'mocks the frailness of her bones,' • enjoys visits: 'leans and snatches/ … gossip' • able to laugh: 'now and then she laughs,'	6	Answers should describe two to three impressions, depending on detail and supporting quotes.

Q	Answer	Mark	Additional Guidance
4.	*Answers may refer to:* • 'shrill' – onomatopoeia – short high sound • 'mirthless laugh' – oxymoron – empty laugh • 'half cough, half whistle' – repetition/ onomatopoeia – wheezy sounds repeated • 'Tuneless and dry as east wind' – simile – monotone/barren/cold • 'through a thistle' – alliteration – hard to voice • 'thistle' – spiky wild plant	4	Best candidates will identify, recognise and explain two uses of language to show insightful understanding of different impressions.
5.	*Answers should include:* • rhyming couplet (whistle/thistle) – cements lines together for impact • use of comma – rhythm broken to mirror ugliness of cough and laugh	3	Rhyme, rhythm and punctuation all to be referred to for 3 marks.
TOTAL		25	

Exercise 1B.8

'Space Invaders' by Owen Sheers

Q	Answer	Mark	Additional Guidance
1.	land: • metaphor: 'dodo waddle' – flightless bird • 'dodo waddle' – staccato sound • onomatopoeia: 'waddle' – sounds clumsy water: • assonance: 'usual smooth cut and groove', 'lakeside glide' – soft smooth long sounds • alliteration: 'soft shoe shuffle' – repeated soft 's' suggests movement • metaphor: 'soft shoe shuffle' – connotations with dance	6	land: award up to 2 marks for techniques or language features with explanations. water: award up to 4 marks for techniques or language features with explanations. Highest marks will go to candidates who explain their choices in detail.
2.	*Answers could include:* • metaphor: 'holsters' – image of cowboy • assonance/metaphor: 'low-slung and puffed' – cowboy image, inflated with self-importance • personification: 'John Wayne swagger' – extending the metaphor • personification: 'menace hinting' – use of 'hinting' • powerful vocabulary: 'dark eyes'	6	Candidates should identify, recognise and explain three for full marks.
3. (a) (b)	• that we should keep our distance *References should be made to:* • silence • threatening • necks • beaks stabbing	1 4	Award 1 mark. Good candidates will rephrase at least two ideas accurately in their own words.

Q	Answer	Mark	Additional Guidance
4.	*Answer should identify:* • 'confront us with beauty and the promise of pain' *Answers should refer to:* • contrasting feelings: wonder and fear • threatening but beautiful, yet may cause pain	4	Award 2 marks for identification. Award 1 mark for interpretation of feelings. Award 1 mark for explanation in own words.
5.	*Answers could include:* • swans invade humans' space • explanation of invasion • poet invades swans' space • assonance: space invaders – the repeated sound draws words together	4	*Marker's discretion* Award marks according to understanding, insight and ability to express ideas.
TOTAL		25	

Exercise 1B.9

'The Hero' by Siegfried Sassoon

Q		Answer	Mark	Additional Guidance
1.		*Answers could include:* • resigned: 'Jack fell as he'd have wished' • controlled: 'something broke/ ... to a choke' • proud: 'We mothers are so proud', 'weak eyes ... gentle triumph', 'he'd been so brave' • sad: 'her face was bowed' • lonely: 'no-one seemed to care/ ... lonely woman'	6	*Marker's discretion* Two impressions should be dealt with in detail. More could be covered in less detail.
2.	(a)	*Suggestions should refer to:* • bravery/patriotism/heroism/flattery about character • to speed up the job/following orders/ wanted an easy life: cynical, hypocritical, cowardly	2	Up to 2 marks for a realistic and thoughtful answer.
	(b)	• out of kindness/felt sorry for her: sympathetic	2	Up to 2 marks for reason and character observation. (NB the 'he'd' in line 7 could be interpreted as referring to the Colonel or the Brother Officer)
3.	(a)	Mother: • proud of her son/thinks he is a hero/ loving towards him Officer: • useless/cowardly/feeble/deserter	2	2 marks for accurate insight on both Mother and Officer.
	(b)	*Answers might include:* • reference to Sassoon's views • message of last two lines • specific vocabulary • understanding of both views	4	Up to 4 marks for an insightful and well-reasoned answer to include supporting evidence.

Q		Answer	Mark	Additional Guidance
4.		*Answers should refer to:* rhythm: • regular • moves it on • predictable • childlike • irony • understates seriousness rhyme: • stanzas 1 and 3: aabbcc • stanza 2: ababcc • some regularity • moves it on • predictable • childlike • irony • understates seriousness	4	Candidates should recognise regularity for 1 mark. Award up to 3 marks for understanding of effect/ form.
5.	(a) (b)	*Answers may refer to:* • true hero • irony – only to mother • hero maybe to some people • title that shows understanding • clear explanation of ideas	2 3	Up to 2 marks for two clearly expressed reasons. Award up to 3 marks for title and explanation, which display originality and understanding.
TOTAL			25	

Exercise 1B.10

'The Lake' by Roger McGough

Q		Answer	Mark	Additional Guidance
1.	(a)	*Answers should refer to:* fearfulness of the park and the lake: • no fish • no birds • vegetation dying and trees growing away from the lake • darkness at night	4	Good candidates should sum up reasons for avoidance. e.g. fear: award 1 mark. Award 3 marks for three points in own words.
	(b)	*Answers might refer to:* • 'like the plague' • keeping distance for fear of contamination • historical context	3	Award 1 mark. Award up to 2 marks for quality and detail of explanation.
2.		*Answers should include:* • pollution increasing: 'pigs breed and multiply' – metaphor • lake filling with rubbish which 'pigs' feed on: 'they live on dead fish and rotting things' – metaphor extended	4	Best candidates will recognise symbolism of pigs and the extended metaphor. *Marker's discretion* Award marks according to understanding and insight of answer.
3.		*Answers could include:* • sadness that lake's pursuits – feeding the ducks, sailing boats, fishing, etc. – are not possible at the lake anymore • irony that outdoor pursuits are now being enacted indoors because of man's pollution • safety from the lake inside – pursuits are now indoor pretence not outdoor reality • mounting rubbish/pollution in houses	4	Reward candidates who display an overall understanding. Good candidates should allude to two points.

Q	Answer	Mark	Additional Guidance
4.	*Answers could include:* • 'drowned pets' – disgust at image • 'putrid' – sound and meaning of word • 'piggy eyes glisten' – greedy eyes/relish • 'acquired a taste for flesh' – shocking • 'licking their lips' – dread of what to come	6	Three words/phrases needed. Reward choice and insight.
5.	*Answers should refer to:* • pollution ruining the environment • man's consumerism and waste	4	Reward understanding, depth and quality of ideas.
TOTAL			**25**

Paper 2: Writing

General guidance for the candidate

ISEB syllabus states:

'Candidates are expected to express themselves clearly and accurately, using standard English spelling, grammar, punctuation, syntax and appropriate vocabulary.'

All compositions for Studied Literature essays and the Writing Tasks – fiction and non-fiction – should demonstrate the acquisition and proficiency of good writing skills: presentation, punctuation and spelling.

Presentation
Handwriting should be consistently well-formed in a clear and sophisticated style with regular sizing and spacing. Care should be taken with the indentation of paragraphs and unnecessary crossing out.

Punctuation
Capital letters should be clearly defined and correctly used. A range of punctuation should be evident and used accurately and clearly to define meaning.

Best candidates will use the comma, semi colon, colon, dashes, brackets and apostrophe with confidence. Dialogue, where used, should be punctuated and laid out accurately.

Spelling
Accuracy is expected but not at the expense of using interesting and sophisticated vocabulary. The spelling of high frequency words and homophones should be sound.

Section A: Studied Literature: Exercises 2A.1–2A.11

Essays on Studied Literature will fall into two categories: response to questions on a theme using a chosen text, or open literature questions that are not thematically tied.

The themes of 'conflict', 'heroes and heroines' and 'relationships' rotate but the marking of essays follows the same guidelines.

These guidelines will also guide the marker of open literature responses as the expectations are the same.

ISEB descriptors – how the examiner will mark

Pupils should use the following descriptors which are supplied to examiners by the ISEB, to assist them in interpreting their marks, and to anticipate expected marks on their performance.

Mark	Descriptors
1–11	Knowledge and understanding of the text(s) not relevant to the task; not clear in terms of organisation; technically very inaccurate; very short and undeveloped.
12–15	Knowledge and understanding of the text(s) generally relevant to the task; some reference to the text made to support ideas; ideas clearly communicated and organised into paragraphs; spelling sufficiently accurate.
16–19	Knowledge and understanding of the text(s) mainly relevant to the task; good reference to the text to develop ideas; ideas clearly communicated; well-structured essay; spelling generally accurate.
20–25	Knowledge and understanding of the text(s) consistently relevant to the task; sound insight shown; close reference to the text to develop ideas fully; ideas clearly communicated; detailed and well-structured essay; spelling generally accurate; a good range of appropriate vocabulary.

Guidelines to aid interpretation of key words in descriptors

Knowledge
Essays should provide a detailed knowledge of the text: plot, characters, setting(s), historical context and author's background.

Understanding
An insight into general issues and themes in the book is essential. Candidates should be able to sift relevant information and apply their understanding to the current theme.

Relevance to the task

An accurate understanding of the question must be proved: constant reference to the demands of the question should be evident. Candidates should take care not simply to retell the story in an attempt to show off what they know.

Reference to text

Best and relevant examples from the chosen text should be used to explain and support statements and ideas. These should be selected appropriately and without repetition.

Care should be taken to include detailed examples yet without irrelevant information.

Ideas clearly communicated

Ideas should be clearly communicated in a convincing way. Candidates should give due consideration to planning and forethought and guide their marker confidently through a well-shaped and logical essay.

Structure

The structure of the essay should show evidence of clear planning and sequencing of ideas. The introduction should state the book(s) and author(s) studied and prove an understanding of the demands of the question.

The main body of the essay should develop a logical and clear progression of ideas with supporting evidence and at all times directly answer the question.

Paragraph breaks should be used purposefully and the progression of ideas within each paragraph should be fluent.

Topic sentences should be used clearly at the beginning of each paragraph with ensuing ideas clearly grouped.

Careful use of transition words (or 'signpost words') will enable the reader to understand the interpretation of the question.

The conclusion will summarise and emphasise the preceding key points.

Spelling

Spelling should be generally accurate, with due care given to words linked to the theme and the characters and places from the chosen book. The correct spelling and punctuation of the book and author is assumed.

Vocabulary

Candidates should display a confident range of vocabulary specifically related to the theme and the characters.

Section B: Writing Task – Fiction and Non-fiction: Exercises 2B.1–2B.12

Definition of question types

Questions/titles will fall broadly into five categories. Some questions/titles expect a fiction response; some expect a non-fiction response. There are some which can be interpreted and written in either way and will be marked accordingly. The following sections are guidelines to help interpret key words from the above ISEB marking grid:

Discursive: Exercise 2B.7

This may be argument or persuasive writing in the form of a letter, speech, article or essay.

Directed: Exercise 2B.8

This may be a response to a quote, a proverb, an excerpt from a poem, a statement or an opening sentence. The form of the essay may fall into any genre depending on the writer's interpretation of the stimulus.

Narrative: Exercise 2B.9

This will be a story written in the first or third person. Writing could be purely fictional or based, to some extent, on personal experience (autobiographical).

Descriptive: Exercise 2B.10

This could be a description of a real or imagined place or person, or both.

Personal: Exercise 2B.11

This could be a piece of writing from personal experience (autobiographical) in the form of a diary, story or description.

Mixed: Exercise 2B.12

There are a number of titles under the heading 'Mixed'. The interpretation, and therefore the form of the response, may fall into any genre.

ISEB descriptors – how the examiner will mark

Pupils should use the following descriptors which are supplied to examiners by the ISEB to assist them in interpreting their marks, and to anticipate expected marks on their performance.

Mark	Descriptors
1–11	Not relevant to the chosen task; clarity weak owing to poor organisation and technical inaccuracy; very short and undeveloped with little attention to detail.
12–15	Generally relevant to the task; ideas clearly communicated and organised into paragraphs; some attention to detail; style and tone generally appropriate for the chosen task; spelling sufficiently accurate.
16–19	Mainly relevant to the task; ideas clearly communicated and well structured in an effective and interesting way; good attention to detail; style and tone adapted well for the chosen task; spelling generally accurate; a good range of vocabulary and expression.
20–25	Consistently relevant to the task; ideas developed fully and well structured in an original and stylish way; excellent attention to detail; essay much enhanced by style and tone; spelling consistently accurate; a wide range of vocabulary and expression.

Guidelines to aid interpretation of key words in descriptors

Fiction and non-fiction are dealt with separately, as the skills needed to effect good writing vary according to each genre.

1. Fiction

When considering the **structure** of fiction writing, the definitions and guidelines for marking are subdivided into narrative and descriptive writing.

Relevance

The essay must be based on the given title with constant and appropriate reference to it.

The genre chosen should be adhered to in style, content and tone.

Ideas

Ideas should reflect creative and original use of the title.

Ideas within the essay should be interesting, thought provoking and engaging.

Structure

The structure of the essay should show clear planning and sequencing of ideas.

Paragraph breaks should be used purposefully and the progression of ideas within each paragraph should be fluent.

Narrative (may include autobiographical writing)

The overall shape of the story should be clear and evident with a strong opening and with a purposeful end in mind.

It could embrace the use of flashback or other stylistic devices.

Candidates should show off their ability to write an interesting and manageable plot with appropriate climax and shape.

There should be sufficient balance between the plot, the description of the characters within it and the setting.

Descriptive (may include autobiographical writing)

The structure of descriptive writing should be clearly evident. The writer's viewpoint, if describing a place, should be established: whether describing a landscape in an organised way from a static position or as if passing through it.

There are various ways to structure the description of character – care should be taken that the piece does not seem disjointed.

Detail

The reader needs to be able to picture his/her surroundings: appropriate setting details ranging from the overview, such as weather and light, to the immediate foreground should be given.

To provide this detail the setting(s) could be explored through a variety of senses.

Characters should be developed in a detailed way to go beyond physical attributes but also to include consistent and believable actions, dialogue, reactions and feelings.

If the chosen writing genre is descriptive, and not narrative, the detail should be greatly enhanced.

If the chosen genre is autobiography the writing should be in the first person and reflect the personality and feelings of the writer.

Style

The candidate's grasp of grammar and syntax should be clear and confident.

Sentence structures should provide a variety of openings: simple, compound and complex sentences should be used appropriately and smoothly according to the context.

Verb tenses should be used accurately and consistently and tense changes used for effect where appropriate.

A range of writing features such as imagery, sound devices and the powerful use of words (e.g. rule of three and repetition) should be used to enhance the composition. This should be particularly evident in the writing of description.

Tone

The tone should enhance the writing and should be appropriate to the genre and audience. Care should be taken with the use of violence, adult issues and innuendo.

The use of a humorous tone should be measured and applicable to all readers.

Spelling

Spelling should be generally accurate with due care given to subject specific words where appropriate. Candidates should not be penalised for misspelling adventurous and sophisticated words.

Vocabulary

A sophisticated, relevant and succinct vocabulary will set apart best candidates. The use of inappropriate slang and modern euphemisms should be avoided.

2. Non-fiction

When considering the structure and style of non-fiction writing, the definitions and guidelines for marking are subdivided into argument, persuasive, diary and recount writing.

Relevance

The essay must be based on the given title with appropriate reference to it.

The genre chosen should be adhered to in style, content and tone.

Ideas

Ideas should reflect creative and original use of the title.

Ideas within the essay should be thought provoking, engaging and, if relevant, informative.

Structure

The structure of the essay should show evidence of clear planning and sequencing of ideas.

Paragraph breaks should be used purposefully and the progression of ideas within each paragraph should be fluent.

Topic sentences should be used clearly at the beginning of each paragraph with ensuing ideas clearly grouped.

The use of transition words (or 'signpost words') is essential to enable the reader to understand the direction of the argument.

A powerful opening and conclusion should be evident.

Argument Writing

This could be in the form of a letter, article or essay.

Argument writing should provide an introduction to outline the topic followed by clear and balanced paragraphs for and against the topic and a conclusion where the writer's opinion may be given if requested.

Persuasive Writing

This could be in the form of a letter, article, essay or speech.

Persuasive writing should provide an arresting opening followed by logical and paragraphed ideas dealing largely with one side of the argument. The conclusion should leave the reader in no doubt as to the opinion of the writer/speaker.

N.B. Letter Writing: the correct placing and spacing of addresses, date and sign off is expected.

Diary Writing

Diary writing may be written in the chronological order of events, may deal with a series of flashbacks or be dictated by the exploration of themes or feelings.

Recount/autobiographical

Recount writing may be structured chronologically or as a result of the themes and emotions explored.

Detail

A clear understanding and knowledge of the subject matter should underpin the writing.

Points should be well explained with supporting evidence or anecdotal reference where appropriate.

Style

Sentence structures should provide a variety of openings; simple, compound and complex sentences should be used appropriately and smoothly according to the context.

Verb tenses should be used accurately and consistently and tense changes used for effect where appropriate.

Argument Writing

Argument writing should be written in the passive tense to provide objectivity. A range of persuasive writing techniques should be evident but used in a moderate way.

Persuasive Writing

Persuasive writing should be written in the active and imperative tenses to convey subjectivity.

A wide range of persuasive writing techniques/features should be evident and used in a forceful or persuasive way. These techniques may include the use of facts and statistics, playing on guilt, use of direct appeals and emotive language. Writing techniques, such as rhetorical questions, rules of three and repetition, should be used to maintain a persuasive style.

Diary writing

Diary writing should be written in the first person. The use of tenses should be consistent but may vary for impact. The reason or stimulus for the diary entry should be inherent and the moods and emotions resulting clearly developed.

The exploration of personal feelings must be strongly evident.

Recount/autobiographical

Autobiographical writing as non-fiction writing may take the form of a recount written in the first person.

A recount may be in the first or third person and is written in the past tense throughout.

Tone

The degree of formality should be appropriate to the genre, subject matter and audience.

The use of a humorous tone should be measured and applicable to all readers.

Spelling

Genre and subject specific words should be spelt accurately.

Vocabulary

An interesting and sophisticated vocabulary specific to the genre should be used.